The Miracle of Gratitude, The Miracle of Life

Copyright © 2014 by Elaine Pace, Denise Appelmans
http://therelinquishment.com

ALL RIGHTS RESERVED. This book contains material protected under International and Federal Copyright Laws and Treaties. Any unauthorized reprint or use of this material is prohibited. No part of this book may be reproduced or transmitted in any form or by any means, electronic or mechanical, including photocopying, recording, or by any information storage and retrieval system without express written permission from the authors.

ISBN: 978-0-9937911-0-9

Published and designed by studio ponnuki
http://ponnuki.net

Table of Contents

Introduction..6

The Teachers...9

Chapter One..15
Raising the Curtain on Gratitude..........................15

Chapter Two..20
Bring Forth the Only Truth, Love..........................20
I ~ Gratitude for the Self..20
II ~ Selflessly Serving the Self...............................23
III ~ The Invocation of Gratitude..........................30

Chapter Three...34
Cleanse the Shadows...34
I ~ Wonderment..34

Chapter Four...44
Call Forth the Energy of the Sacred......................44
I ~ Intention...45
II ~ Acceptance...50
III ~ Peace...60
IV ~ Love...65
V ~ Celebration!..72
Epilogue..78
The Miracle of this Book...78
Daily Teachings..82

Acknowledgment..86

The Miracle of Gratitude, The Miracle of Life

*Gratitude calls forth the energies of the sacred,
brings forth a cleansing of the shadows
and brings forth the only truth, love.*

−*Nathan*

Introduction

Imagine this! One day you are living what is considered a relatively normal life, nothing exemplary, with challenges, joys, questions, answers, ups and downs. There are many ways in which you think your life could be a whole lot better, but overall you are aware of your progress, blessings, and valuable life experience. You have a sense that you know what is going on in life and that as much as possible you are on top of things. You wish many of your struggles would vanish, however you have come to accept the daily grind. You have contemplated change, however ruled it out because it just might make things worse. After all, your life has been like this for a long time. Yet your restless mind cannot be quieted.

The next day when you least expect it, something miraculous occurs and your life is never the same again. What do you do? What do you think? How do you respond?

Over two years ago, this happened to me. I received a most extraordinary and deeply touching gift of connecting with Divine Teachers in Spirit, in a conscious, interactive way. They reached right into my life and began speaking to me through my friend, who is an intuitive. Not only did this occur once. The interaction evolved over two years, and still goes on today. Talk about a miracle! I call it "the miracle of gratitude – the miracle of love."

This came as a complete surprise, or as one would say, out of the blue. Consciously, this was not something I was seeking, anticipating, or even imagining. Yet now I recognize that there had long been a yearning in my heart to experience love in its truest form, freedom to live the life that is authentically mine and a sense of fulfillment of the purpose for which I was created.

At a significant crossroads in my life, I knew that something had to change. Simply put, I knew I had to find a better way to live. There were many aspects of my life in which I felt confined, restricted and totally void of joy. Over time I felt I was living a lie. Deep inside I knew something had to shift, or life was not worth living. Occasionally depression turned to despair and hopelessness. I did everything in my power to conceal this from others, yet my body did not lie. I engulfed myself in excess weight and was miserable. I felt disconnected from others. Home did not seem like home to me anymore. I lost touch with my heart.

In dark moments, I called out to the heavens for help. Not sure whom I was addressing, I made a desperate and persistent plea. Looking back, I see this was a summons of sorts and a powerful one at that. It was also a declaration that something had to happen in the form of a release from my self-imposed prison, so that I could live as never before. Specifically, I wanted to feel well, alive, like I had something worthwhile to contribute to humankind. I sensed I had something to offer. I just didn't know what.

I began to feel a stirring in my heart to write a book. I thought of co-authoring the book with my close friend, Denise, the intuitive, whom I had so often consulted for guidance and wisdom. I imagined writing letters to her with questions about life and she would reply by drawing on her intuitive abilities to provide answers from Spirit. Having worked for many years in the mental health field, I was well acquainted with people's stories about the jagged areas of their lives. I engaged with people who could not always heal their deep emotional scars and wounds. This evoked many questions in them and in me. So I viewed this book as a potential source of understanding and relief. How my heart leapt with excitement when I shared my ideas with Denise and discovered she was in full agreement. Although we seemed to be on the same wavelength, neither of us acted upon this idea for well over a year.

It took the prompting of repeated dreams for both of us to acknowledge it was time to begin. What occurred, though, was something far different than either of us ever anticipated. Instead of receiving and sharing guidance in the typical manner of her intuitive readings, Denise suddenly emerged in the role of transmitter for Teachers in Spirit. This meant that as I sat with Denise after centering ourselves and breathing deeply, one Teacher or another conversed with me, through Denise.

These Ascended Masters, (spiritual masters who once walked the earth) as we were to discover, had a whole curriculum ready for us. They brought forth ancient teachings of love, which we were to learn experientially in a manner that would transform our lives. We were then asked to share this material with the world. We had no idea what we were in for!

The Teachers

The first Teacher to speak to me had a deep voice reflecting a male presence, an Ascended Master who is actively bringing forth the teachings of love upon this planet. His name is Nathan. I met Nathan the very first time Denise and I sat down to gather material for our book. We sat across from one another to do a reading, however within moments I knew someone else was speaking to me, because of things said about ancient times, different vocabulary used, and concepts conveyed which Denise claimed to know nothing about. "Nathan", as he asked us to call him, introduced me to teachings I had never heard before.

While no words adequately describe his gentle presence, his love, his wisdom, his steadfastness, or his extreme brilliance, I will tell you about my experience of being his student.

Within weeks of meeting Nathan and beginning to receive the teachings, I was given an experience of love so profound that I did not know what to do with myself. Nathan reached right inside of me, bypassing all my protective mechanisms to engage my trembling heart. I felt as if I was a scared, lonely child hiding in the closet, who was extended a hand of love and tender encouragement to come forth. All my defenses crumbled, as I experienced an emotional release akin to a tsunami.
I have never in my life known such love.

Accompanying this was a flash of awareness that there is tremendous love pouring forth from those in Spirit, to all who inhabit our planet. I had no idea that this was the case, to such an extent. The impact of this revelation on my life was huge. I knew that no matter what my life circumstances are, I am always loved and am never alone. Further, I knew unequivocally that there is a divine order in existence. For even though I observe chaos, crime, poverty, war and devastation throughout the world, I am also aware of and influenced by the presence of love, generosity, joy, and the striving for peace and equality.

This divine order is reflective of the universal love pouring upon us from the source of all love, the Omnipotent. It is reflective of a far broader purpose and plan than I will ever know. Even though I may think that our planet is headed for destruction, I know there is a huge influx of love supporting humankind so that we can save the planet and ourselves.

All the teachings that came my way and will be shared over time are teachings of love, which upon being applied in our lives will change the face of humankind. This is more than an expansion of consciousness. It is an actual change in perspective, to warrant a radical change in the way we live. No one will be left out. No one will be excluded. In other words, over time everyone on the planet will be affected in one way or another by what is occurring as we learn about, implement, and are transformed by living a life of gratitude and love.

The time is at hand for an enormous shift from living in separation, inequality, prejudice, and misery, to living in love, recognizing our unity with one another, and realizing the resources of the planet are to be shared by all. I have been told there is urgency for humankind to embrace ourselves in the most authentic, loving way possible. There is to be no compromise. We are to make it happen. Peace on earth will only occur as love flourishes. There is no other way.

The more the Teachers guided me, probed my heart and mind with questions, challenged me with tasks, imparted their wisdom to me, the more the truth of each of their many teachings began to reverberate within. The words of the Masters resonated so powerfully that I began to see things differently and effect far-reaching change.

As the weeks and months progressed, I found there is such great depth to the teachings that I needed to revisit them many times to grasp them on all levels.
Time was needed for integration. However, regardless of what I understood at the time, or how often a teaching was thoughtfully presented to me for review, I knew that what The Teachers were saying was true. I knew it in every fiber of my being. My mind knew it, and it also registered in my body as a felt knowing. As it is said, "the body never lies." My whole being poured forth its assent. Still, it was not always easy to make sense of and incorporate the teachings into my life. I had intense times of struggle and pain as I peeled off the layers of my protective façade, resisted the truth, and ground in my heels of stubbornness.

Throughout all this, Nathan loved, supported and held me. I was always accepted and always loved. Time and time again I was reminded that this entire experience is not for me alone. I am a representative of the human nation, learning in order to pass along these precious teachings, which reaffirms my awareness of the unconditional love that pours forth over us all.

Nathan soon introduced another master to me. This master, whose name is Mother, came forth to teach gratitude and many other aspects of love. While Nathan represents a more global love, Mother comes forth with a mother's consciousness, not unlike that of a lioness!

Filled with love, Mother is razor sharp with her words and always cuts to the heart of the matter. She leaves no stone unturned. Mother is the primary teacher of gratitude and is passionate about her teachings. I soon realized in working with her, that She will not rest until humankind learns what we need to learn, to live in love.
I experience her as unflinching in her determination to bring forth true gratitude in me, and all of humankind. For in doing so, She ushers in the age of love.

Mother appears to never rest, never stop. Mother gets what she wants.
In our work, Mother has pushed me to my limits time and time again. Just when I thought I could not take my next step because it was grueling and beyond my reach, She gave me exactly what I needed in the form of loving encouragement, clarity, and understanding. It very often felt like being on a roller coaster ride. Repeatedly, Mother explained that She reflects back to me the call of my heart, and the way I can answer that call, so my life can be lived exactly as it is intended to be. Mother is relentless in her call to each one of us to embrace the fullness of the beauty and richness of ourselves. I would lay myself at her feet in an instant!

Encountering divine teachers for two years of learning has been unlike anything I have ever experienced. I cannot emphasize enough that the love I have met with is unparalleled and universal. It is also uncompromising. The Teachers explained that,

"We are very close to you. Nay to judge and watch you - to comfort you, to give love, to protect, to surround all around you, and hold your heart. That is always only our duty. Religion will say that we are there to judge. We will never judge you. Religion will say we are there to give command for you to be obedient and nay to have your own will. That is folly! We are there to comfort, to protect." *

I experience that love, profoundly, in the most liberating ways imaginable. The teachings evoke a continual calling forth of the truth of my being, including my shadows and my light. The Teachers allow me to see my potential, the gifts I have to offer, and what to do to move beyond anything that deceives me. I have had the opportunity to experience all facets of myself, in the presence of divine beings who know me more thoroughly than I will ever know myself. Working with the Teachers can be likened to immersion in the most comprehensive course on how to live my most authentic, and therefore most fulfilling life.

These teachings are not intended to remain with me though. I was told that I am a representative of the human nation, and although experiencing the beauty, the intensity and the subsequent transformation of this series firsthand, my mission is to bring it forth into the world. The teachings are coming to the earth in a timely manner. Nathan explained that we're approaching a time of the opening of the consciousness of love, and that the full impact is beginning here on this planet, now. He stated that,

This love is not the love of which mankind thinks (pleasure). It's a love of all, and a love of connection and a love of universal authority. It's a love of passionately embracing all nations, all beings, all people, all. It is about all people feeling love.

It's time now for these teachings to come forward so that people can understand that if the consciousness of man does not shift itself toward the higher calling of love, we will drift from the shores of ourselves, only to sink in the sadness that we've created.

I was told that *the root of peace is Love*. It is imperative that humankind accepts the call to love as never before. The teachings of love, however, begin with the teachings of gratitude, for without gratitude love cannot exist. Gratitude is the topic of this book and even though it may seem that everything you need to know about gratitude is included here, this is only the richest of beginnings. These teachings will be expanded upon in subsequent e-books, as gratitude is intertwined with the other teachings like a vibrantly coloured thread dancing through a tapestry.

With humble love and gratitude in my heart for my gracious Teachers, I share their teachings of gratitude with you.

* The words that are in ***bold italics*** in this book are direct quotes from The Teachers.

Chapter One

Raising the Curtain on Gratitude

Upon hearing that living in gratitude is vital and essential for bringing forth love, I immediately wondered what the difference is between gratitude, and saying "thank you." Nathan told me that

Gratitude is beyond thank you. It is from the depths of your being. Gratitude is the essential essence of honouring the spark within another. When gratitude is present, in all four of the parts of the whole (acceptance, peace, intention and love), when gratitude is given upon the opening of the eye and upon the closure of the eye, before a feast or famine, before water or sand, when before a drunken man or before the birth of a child, it calls forth the energies of the sacred, it brings forth a cleansing of the shadows and brings forth the only truth, love.

I was fascinated to hear this, and realized there is a lot to learn about gratitude.

From what Nathan shared, I could see that living with gratitude is so much more than saying thank you for a kindness or gift or a wonderful day. It incorporates deep respect for my fellow human being by acknowledging the spark or light within them and bringing it forth. It puts us all on an even playing field. What also excited me in this teaching was the vast transformational properties of gratitude. There was way more here than I anticipated, and I was eager to find out more about it. I wanted to apply what I was learning to see where it would take me.

I had often thought of gratitude as a warm feeling in response to obvious blessings, or great fortune, such as when someone who was ill recovered, or when a friend got a job she really wanted, or when I overcame an obstacle in life and felt great. Even witnessing the marvels of nature could easily elicit a feeling of gratitude. Nathan indicated that there is far more to gratitude than feeling good in response to things I like or am seemingly in alignment with. Of course that is part of it, but it goes further than that.

Mother explained that *gratitude is an active principle*. As time went on, I came to understand it as a way of life or response to life. I was taught many aspects of living in gratitude that I saw as revolutionary. My view of the world was turned upside down, and many of my tried and true ways were gradually relinquished in favour of living in an entirely new way. All this led to the deeper discovery of many aspects of myself which I had never known before, and then beyond that, to the joy of fully being myself.

To begin with, I was faced with incorporating gratitude into my life when I seldom had a sunny disposition. As a young retiree, I was emotionally up and down like a roller coaster. I felt like a fish out of water without my career, and wondered what I was supposed to do with my life, whether or not I had any worth without a professional identity, and whether I now had to reinvent myself. I felt as if I had led myself into an abyss. I hadn't previously realized how much my worldview included the notion that I had to *be somebody* or *do something worthwhile* in order to be viewed as or feel okay in the world. What was I to do with my life and myself now? There were few bright moments as I grappled with these questions.

Naturally I wondered whether practicing gratitude when I was tense or anxious or pessimistic or angry, was even possible. Of course there was an element of stubbornness that typically infiltrated my emotions at any given time, so I was not predisposed to letting go – even of a bad mood. Now I was being taught that gratitude. . . **brings forth a cleansing of the shadows and brings forth the only truth, love.** Deep within me I knew I needed these teachings in order to make it through the remainder of my life with any degree of joy, meaning, and long-term mental health.

Many a day I delved into all this on my routine walk. As I trudged along an isolated forest road, brewing in a swirl of debilitating thoughts and emotions, I mustered everything I could to express gratitude. I had to voice it aloud for some reason, in the crisp outdoor air, with only my poodle to hear me. There ensued a bit of a struggle. On the one hand I observed some relief creeping in as I expressed gratitude for my life, my surroundings, my inner battles, and much more. On the other hand I was invested in the story I had created about my life, which fuelled the fire of my emotions. The story was primarily the litany of events from my past which had challenged me and which I had resisted.

It became my reason or rationale for unhappiness, instead of my backdrop for opportunity. Regardless of what crept into my mind, I persisted in expressing gratitude for all that was.

Nathan encouraged me to continue to express gratitude, and to express it for myself. I was told gratitude is called for (repeatedly) during dark times. When I indicated that it was most difficult to express gratitude for my life when I was in a state of upheaval, I was told to say:

"I have glorious gratitude for me!" before going to bed at night, and upon waking in the morning.

"For me?" I enquired.

Yes!

When I actually started doing that, the teachings on gratitude began to take on more meaning. Gratitude for myself led me into a whole new world. As I tentatively ventured forth, I observed that living in gratitude for me during dark times gave me the reassurance that there is a loving presence with me. Connecting with that loving presence soothed my entire being.

Somehow, though, I needed to be more in sync with myself before I could allow that loving presence to fully embrace me. When encountering difficulties it was all too easy to deflect love in favour of my self-limiting thoughts. Nathan taught me how to move beyond this by cultivating gratitude and "excavating" my true self.

Find the authentic self. This is done by love. The authentic self is not about a job, or the expression of the self, nor is it about living in love –authenticity IS love. Do you love who you are with, inside of you and outside of you? Do you love who you are in the day in which you live? Do you love the person you are at the end of the day? Do you love the person you are at the beginning of the day? Do you stand in front of your reflection in the mornings, and before you even cleanse your face say "I love you", or do you look for a blemish or a wrinkle?

And partway through your day do you stop and look at your hands that have served you continuously and say, "My! I am so grateful for you. You serve me, you feed me, you touch the suffering, you help me to feel my world. Thank You! I am so grateful for you".

And at the end of your day do you look into the mirror and have gratitude that you have had a whole day - a whole day - to see the sun, to see the stars, to see those you love and those you don't, to laugh, to eat, to breathe? Life is not complex, humans are. Life is as simple as what I have just told you, and living from that place of gratitude, for those simple moments.

I could see that those simple moments that make up each day are far more precious then I realized. As I began to apply this teaching I felt some of the harshness in my heart dissipate. It then became easier for me to relax. I wondered if this was what Nathan meant by saying that *gratitude. . . calls forth the energies of the sacred.* It was clear that gratitude also calls forth the fullness of life.

Chapter Two

Bring Forth the Only Truth, Love

I ~ Gratitude for the Self

Repeatedly The Teachers taught me to be grateful for myself. I did not understand what they meant at first. It seemed contrary to be grateful for myself unless I had accomplished something outstanding or recognized an exemplary trait. Growing up I was taught to put others ahead of myself. I was told not to get in the way of others nor be in any way an imposition. Early on I learned to relegate myself to the back of the room, so to speak. In time, I automatically assumed that I held an inferior position to most people. Although I was accepting of that to some extent, it resulted in dullness of my being. It also led to an array of compulsive behaviors, including overeating and overspending.

This perception led to two things. First of all, I automatically assumed the position of caregiver for those around me. Secondly, I concluded that I did not have a say in how I live my life. Very much like my mother, I adopted the persona of a martyr. This affected absolutely every decision I made in my life.

Now I was being taught by Divine Teachers to love and be grateful for myself. They said to honour and call forth the fullness of the self. However was I to do this? How was I to embrace an entirely new way of conceiving of myself, my value, and that of everyone around me? In my quiet moments I also asked "Why?" Why does it matter that I love and have gratitude for myself? Could I not love others without loving me? I almost thought there was something wrong about unequivocally loving myself.
Mother addressed this. She began by saying that gratitude for the self is essential because without it, love, acceptance, or peace cannot exist. If I do not love myself, my love of others will be shadowed. The discord within from a lack of self-love and gratitude will sooner or later manifest as discord with others. If this were not enough on an individual basis, it becomes even more explosive between groups of people and nations. Mention was also made of the possibility of creating illness in the body if I fed myself with dislike or hatred, persistently, over time.

Gratitude for the self opens the pathway to love. In its refined state, this is gratitude for the light within. It affords an individual a safe place to call home: the human heart. When gratitude and love are present for the self in this way, there exists a sense of security that is unshakable. Possibilities for joy are endless.

If I deny myself gratitude and love, it is likely that I will deny the true expression of my gifts and the fulfillment of my potential. Mother explained that if I hold back my light, or my gifts, or the contribution I am here to make, I deny not only myself, but the world as well. She referred to the entire human race as the "unified whole." She stated:

When you do not allow this to be, you are denying the unified whole an essential piece, a part of its completion. If all parts are to be integrated, all parts must be present. If you deny your truest expression, even in the moment, you are denying the unified whole.

Where then can another who is truly struggling, for example with their earthbound mother, find a way to say, "I cannot! I can only be me."

Do you see?

"Yes, yes, I do," I asserted.

Where, where is it within the human nation that it takes one to say "enough"?

Not for something grand and world changing, but in that instant of a moment, the smallest moments.

I was beginning to see the picture, yet I needed to know more. I asked how I could overcome my hesitation about allowing my truest expression, and to fully come forth in the world. This led to the next teaching.

II ~ *Selflessly Serving the Self*

Mother acquainted me with a teaching that completely turned my world upside down. It was a teaching that I needed to learn my entire life. I also wished that my family members, particularly my mother, had known this as well. What I learned essentially gave me back my life, restored a feeling of empowerment, and set me free to live my life fully. It did not occur overnight, though, because I was like a young child newly starting out in kindergarten. I stumbled a lot.

In Mother's words:

Every human is responsible to the self in order to give selfless service. There must be a complete way of being "selfless to the self" to be selfless to another. When you live from the fear of another, you are self-serving, not selfless to the self. But when you embrace your palpable enthusiasm and you state it, and you act upon your truth, it is as if you are serving another in the most selfless way. You are truly giving to the most authentic, essential part of yourself without thought for the self. It just simply is. If you are to deny that, then what you are doing is serving the self in a selfish way.

From that I understood that love necessitates selflessly serving the self. In order to selflessly serve others, I am to first give to myself in a selfless way. I learned that selfless service to the self involves complete regard for the truth of who I am, what I need, and what I desire. "Selfless", I was taught, means to give to the self out of love instead of fear. Giving to myself in this manner results in a "filling of the tank", instead of a depletion of personal resources.

As Mother spoke, I thought of ways that this plays out in the work setting. I recalled my time in the work force, and that if someone asked me to take on an additional assignment I would most often say "yes" against my better judgment. As I did so I would feel myself raging inside, because I already had all the work I could handle. Yet, because I was intimidated by some of my colleagues, I did not want to assert myself and say "no". Consequently, I would grit my teeth, proceed with the assignment, and feel stressed, resentful, and angry toward myself. By allowing a sense of inferiority to prevail, I denied myself my voice and peace of mind. This was clearly serving the self in a selfish way. I was acting out of fear.

Had I said to my colleague that I was not available to take on the assignment and instead offer some ideas about how it could have been done, I would have been serving the self in a selfless way. That would likely have contributed to greater harmony in the office setting, and in me. Perhaps relating in this way over time would also have reduced my high blood pressure!

I wanted to know more about selflessly serving the self in everyday life, so requested an example.

Mother continued:

Let us look at everyday life. You are walking along a path and you have happened upon another person. You look at one another. Ah! The protocol of a human is that you smile. Meanwhile inside you are sad. The protocol of a human is that you say "And how are you today?" The protocol of the human is that you put yourself aside and interact - oh, be kind, socialize, share a glass of wine. But inside, your being is screaming, "No! Not today. I want to be alone, not to be busy. I do not wish to put my self aside to know about you."

Yet you choose to follow the protocol. Why? Because you are serving the self, because you are afraid of being abandoned, you are afraid they may not like you, you are afraid you are not there for them, you are afraid of so many things. All about you.

But if it is selfless, then you are completely honoring your vibration of truth, which taps the truth of the other, and you both, on the path, have an opportunity to interact in the purest of ways.

If you were to be in a place of selfless service to the self, and you are on the path, and the other being is coming to you, and you simply raise your eyes and say from your soul, "I love you", and you continue; if the other being so chooses to react and demand, they have a chance to learn to be selfless, for a selfless being would understand that the other is in service of the self. It is a complete interaction of selfless service for all.

Often selfless service is seen as renunciating parts of the self to kneel, and prostrate and serve another, but over time the one in service begins to wonder inside, "What about me?" Begins to sacrifice their truths. "Perhaps today I have no desire to take your fevered brow into its healing place. I cannot. I am too weak."

Yet selfless service means that you go forth and cleanse the brow of the suffering. What then does that caretaker bring? More suffering to the brow of the suffering. Where is the healing? Where?

"It's absent," I ventured.

It becomes a continuum of suffering. Over time the selfless servant starts to fall apart. The body becomes sick. The mind becomes sick. The being becomes sick. And it always becomes adoration of the self, always. But it is not to indulge.

It is not about a process in which now you are stronger, better, and able to walk less time without your woes.

It is about realizing that when you do as <u>you did</u>, you are serving the self in a selfish way.

Mother was referring to an incident that had occurred a few nights before. I interacted with someone and felt uncomfortable and even threatened by what was asked of me. I became fearful, and instead of stating my truth I completely disregarded myself. I said things I did not want to say and omitted the things I wanted to say. Walking away from the interaction, I felt as if I had let myself down. During the night this feeling escalated into intense anger toward myself.

Mother then asked me what would have been the approach of selfless service to the self. As I told her that I was completely thrown by the interaction, She responded that She did not want to hear my excuses, nor be drawn into my story. She explained that the human tendency is to draw another into the story so that another feels sorry for you. We then commiserate with one another. (In my case that kind of conversation typically added fuel to the fire.) When another feels sorry for me, they are doing me no good. They are neither selflessly serving themselves, nor me.

When asked to describe selfless service to the self in the recent interaction, I noted that honesty would have made an entire difference. I needed to speak my truth, yet I kept silent.

Mother agreed, adding: *Always with love, of course. Are you,* Mother asked, *when you speak your truth with love, saying it to the other person in a pointed way to correct them?*

I thought about this. "No, that is not the case," I replied. "I'm saying it to share my truth in the moment."
That is when it comes forth as love. But when it is to correct another or to place another in alignment with yourself, then it is becoming war.

What else? She asked me. *Continue with your observation.* "In addition to stating my truth, I could have stayed with what felt really right for me, and at the conclusion of the interaction I would have felt more peaceful, and gone peacefully into my night."

There would be no explosion, because you are selflessly serving the self. Tell me Dear One, in your life journey, have you ever had to tend to another person as if in selfless service?

I immediately thought of my mother. "Yes, I have," I commented.

After some time you do so begrudgingly. "I am sick and tired of caring for you. I cannot stand this anymore." There can even come the time when their physical body repulses you.

When it comes to such a heavy hurt, why does that happen?

"It happens because the truth of being myself has been put aside."

It becomes projected on the other person.

"And a loss of love then…"

Precisely! Do you see what I am teaching you?

"Ah, yes," I said, smiling by now.

I thought back to my teenage years, growing up with a mother who was depressed. In many ways I was her caregiver and hated this role. I felt I had no choice but to try to somehow make her feel better. It never worked. In retrospect I realize I was giving to my mother but not giving to me. Selflessly serving the self would have meant that I recognized what I could and couldn't do, what I wanted to do and didn't want to do, and that it was fine to search for help elsewhere. Selflessly serving the self would also have meant doing the things I loved to do, to balance the difficult times I had in the home.

You are still to honor yourself, but perhaps find a way to honor the mother too.

There are times when one must mutually meet another. Do you see how this would bring peace to the human nation?

I could certainly see how it would bring peace to the human heart and peace to all. Living this way would change so much. Exploring relationships, Mother continued with examples of what one might be aching to say.

"Dear Mother, I cannot be what you need me to be. I may not give you a grandbaby during my lifetime. I may not be able to be the married woman you wish me to be. I may not be able to be all the things that you were not, that you asked me to be."

"Dear Mother, I cannot keep my home as you wish. . . . I cannot compensate, Mom, for you. My heart cries because I am always likened to others, who have given baby and life. But I am you, the spirit in you that did not fly; it is in me. 'Tis why I came to you: to fly to heights that you were scared of, so we could both fly. Do you understand me now? Will you relieve me of my suffering so I may selflessly serve myself?" says a child to a mother.

Who is the child who is speaking to you?, She asked me. *Your own.*

"Yes."

I have spoken the words of your child. Not only the child from your womb, dear Woman, but the child in your heart. Did not the child in your heart wish to say all that your daughter has said to you?

"Dear Mother, I cannot have a conventional family. I cannot have a child, or grandbabies as you expect. I cannot be a scholar. I cannot be grand. I cannot be tiny and perfect. I cannot be all that you ask. I cannot. I can be me though! And I am beauty. I am all that you wished you could ever be, mom. Perhaps different, but the essence is similar. If I can selflessly serve me, I have selflessly served you."

Free the child within you, Woman, free your child within! All mothers carry pain, but all mothers can also heal.

As Mother spoke it seemed as if something long frozen within was beginning to thaw. Her words evoked in me a permission of sorts, to not only accept myself but also to set myself free. I knew this had to involve selflessly serving myself, so as to be in selfless service to all.

III ~ *The Invocation of Gratitude*

The graciousness of the Divine knows no bounds. From the onset of interacting with The Teachers, I was met with deep and abiding love. I felt humble as I felt the impact of this, and realized again and again that this love is always there for us.

I love talking to these Spirits! I cherish these Teachers. They have lifted me into a world of recognition of truth and love. The Teachers have a way of gently moving me past my fears and defensiveness, reaching right inside my core, and imbuing me with the most wonderful sensation of unity and belonging. At the same time, I am often fraught with nervousness mingled with excitement, and eagerness to learn tempered with stubbornness, as I proceed through our sessions.

Over time, I attempted to predict what I would be taught by these all-knowing Teachers, and to imagine what would be asked of me. Many a time I trembled at the Teachers' requests. Being a representative of the human nation, I was not only taken through an entire gamut of human emotion and experience; my very foundation was shaken loose! Tried-and-true concepts were blown apart. Some relationships even turned upside down or terminated. I was like a ship tossed about at sea during an unrelenting storm.

The storm had a purpose though. A far-reaching shakeup was necessary for me to peel away the layers of my façade so that I could more fully live in truth. I doubt whether I would have initiated this intense process of change myself. Without the all-encompassing love of the teachers and their revolutionary teachings, I would likely have become cynical, unhealthy and dispassionate. Instead, I am opting for prosperity, love, and longevity!

Although it may be assumed that learning, healing and growth occurred when I was in the presence of the Teachers, most of it took place outside the sessions. It was then that I worked hard to assimilate what I had been taught. It was then that I test drove new concepts and applied whatever I could. This did not occur overnight. I was often propelled into heavy resistance bordering on resentment at times, before finding my way to the truth of what I needed to know and assimilate. What I discovered was that each teaching has many levels, however once a teaching takes root, it finds its own pathway.

There were periods of time when I thought I would never get specific things I was taught. Certain teachings seemed to be perpetually beyond my reach. Oh how I struggled with this! I lost many a night's sleep over it. I always found, though, that no matter how long it took, I would eventually grasp the lesson, even in part. The Teachers told me repeatedly that they *are not asking for perfection*. I was once told that I may be like a bird, crashing into a building and falling to the ground, only to have to get up, dust off my wings, and fly away again. That described my experience of transformation perfectly.

As The Teachers led me through this period of concentrated learning and change, they also consistently offered me the tools I needed, to navigate the journey. Their timing was impeccable; their insight into what I needed, superlative.

One such gift was given in the form of invocations. These matched the teachings in such a way as to call forth exactly what I needed at the time. Reciting these invocations on a daily basis and committing them to memory, was akin to having my own treasure chest. The invocations act as a "glue" of sorts, binding the heart to the essence of the teachings. They draw forth what they signify. They are a tangible expression of divine love.

The Invocation of Gratitude, given by Mother, is a striking example of this. It incorporates the foundation of gratitude for living in love, in selfless service to the self and to others. The more I use this invocation, the more I experience lightness of mood and increased optimism. It serves as a reminder of where I want my focus to be. I invite you to use this invocation often, to commit it to memory and see what it brings forth in you in your day-to-day life.

The Invocation of Gratitude

It is with gratitude that I exist in my love
It is with gratitude that I embrace my heart
It is with gratitude that I satisfy all my desires
It is with gratitude that I give selflessly to the self first
For only then am I truly in selfless service to all
It is with gratitude I live MY LIFE.

Chapter Three

Cleanse the Shadows

I ~ Wonderment

The greatest way that we can express our gratitude in the world, is to share our own personal journey with another; to be a teacher by the way in which you live your life. Not of perfection, but of adventure. Not of sacred holy vows, but of only one vow and that is to be the light that you have been given to be. Gratitude is always the catalyst for the greatest growth and teachings of which you as humankind can experience, and its most sacred place is found only in this moment. Ah! Complete! Then, that moment. Ah! Complete. And that moment.

This teaching from Mother about living in the present moment with gratitude and its promise of transformation astonished me. How could the practice of something so seemingly simple reap such huge rewards? Living in the present moment was not the way I typically lived my life.

I realized that I spend so much time attempting to live, navigate, and manipulate the future, that I rob myself of life now. Much of the mental pain and anguish that I experienced in life resulted from leaping out of the present moment into what I imagine the future to be. Tremendous emotional energy has been poured into picturing possible events and experiences that would result in disadvantage or harm. The grand word for this is worry! I can catapult well beyond worry, though. I have been known to be a drama queen at the best of times, and can conjure up the wildest scenarios, replete with the most outrageous details.

For example, I have never been to a southern destination my entire life, let alone go on a cruise. Recently, on a whim, I decided to knock the ball out of the park and book myself onto a Caribbean cruise, out of Florida. Since then I have been mentally living more in the week of the cruise, than in the present moment. I have been imagining all kinds of scenarios, ranging from exotic and perfect, to mistaken and dangerous. The crowning glory was an overpowering conclusion I arrived at that we could well be shipwrecked (The Titantic), be lost at sea (Life of Pi) and if lucky, one or two of us would end up on a desert island, (Castaway) where we may or may not be found! After entertaining this briefly I decided it was better to remain in the present moment and enjoy what is at hand right here, right now, and let the future, cruise and all, take care of itself!

Even picturing desirable outcomes, to the extent that I am not living in gratitude in the present moment, denies the gifts available to me right now. How tremendously freeing it is to pull back the wild stallions of my mind from surging toward predictions of any kind, and to come back to the present moment.

Mother continued:
As a nation of humans there is a propensity for you to move in the direction of needing to have wisdom of what is from tomorrow, and the next decade, and the next century. You as a human nation always feel secure in your knowing, but it is the knowing that creates the insecurity. It is gratitude that creates the ultimate security. When you are in this moment fully, and you are completely grateful, even in a silent unconscious way, you are the wisest of all beings. Your world is your servant. Your master is the profound wisdom within. And you are unified and whole.

As I listened to Mother speak it dawned on me that I do not know where I will be living five months from now. I am currently in a lovely home surrounded by gardens to delight the senses. The house is only available to me until Springtime. Numerous people in this small community have asked me where I will live when I vacate the house. I tell them," I don't know!" I have some ideas in mind about where I may live, but nothing is certain. This is the first time in 30 years that I have not had a plan mapped out for where I will be in the year ahead. It is very easy and even tempting to jump ahead of myself and construe a plan, but based on what? I know it is not yet time for that. All of this is in the realm of the unknown. Overall, I am content to leave it there.

Being taught that security is in gratitude, not in knowing, seemed foreign at first but then upon reflection, hugely liberating. Is society not always pressing me to gain knowledge, and to be certain about so much? Just when I think I know, I can be proven wrong. There is a certain pressure involved in having to know so much, so consistently, about my life or life at large. For some, this pressure translates into amassing unwanted credentials. For others, it involves searching out every possible means of finding the "right way", even if that translates into ignoring the call of the heart. Upon hearing this teaching, I knew I was ready to relinquish the need to know what was ahead of me all the time, and to embrace gratitude and the present moment more fully. I had had enough of worrying and trying to be in control all the time.

Mother spoke further of how to live in gratitude in the present moment:

If in that moment pain comes forth, perhaps a human interaction, perhaps a grievous moment, or perhaps the promptings of a taunting mind, it is your responsibility as a human to pull yourself into this moment; to look at a tree and say, "'Tis! Such beauty. How can you be so old, so wise, and be here for me to see?"

And in so doing to begin to move your consciousness to "wonderment". You see, gratitude opens the doorway for ultimate wonderment; to live in awe of all that is around you; to live in utter disbelief that such beauty can exist, including yourself.

When another witnesses the beauty in you, they are witnessing the glory of love. When you deny that, when you allow your human self to say "Me? 'Tis not I," you have shut the door to your deepest wisdom. And you have denied your sacred presence, as well as the potentiality to reflect that love on others, and to ignite their own love within themselves. It's a very greedy thing to do!

When you allow yourself to slip into wonderment, do not identify the tree.

"Ah! It is this kind" according to your world's teachings. Or the bird you see, or the wild animal. Merely observe. You have met children who do not know the name of things, have you not?

"Yes, for sure," I replied.

There are many things you do not know the name of. And is it not the most wonderful thing to not know? Is it not the most liberating thing when another human says to you, "And what is your mission on the planet?"

And you look at them and simply say, "I don't know. Perhaps I am doing that right now in speaking to you. That is my mission. Yes! Thank you."

Wonderment is a great catalyst for simplicity. Simplicity is wonderment made manifest in an active form. It begins to have life, a heartbeat, an action. It takes form. Yet it is still not definable, or identifiable, but it has more of a presence.

I had been following Mother up to this point, however did not understand what she meant by her last few remarks on simplicity.

"Will you explain to me," I asked, "what is meant by simplicity being wonderment made manifest in active form?"

That is for you to figure out, She said. *Ponder this and the meaning will come to you.*

In the days to follow I went over her words again and again. I could not figure them out at all. Finally, one evening I was very restless and unable to focus on my writing. I decided to go for a walk to reawaken my creativity. Heading out into the cold, dark, winter's night, I invited Mother to accompany me on my walk and to teach me along the way.

Trudging along in the stillness of the darkened streets, I recalled a recent request I made of Mother, when I asked her how I could be more aware of her loving arms around me in my day-to-day life. At the time I had been feeling quite vulnerable and not entirely on my game.

She had replied: *Simple! It is very easy for you to know I am there. It is for you to put your loving arms around yourself, and when your mind tells you a story to make you sad, you tell your mind, "Mother is here, and is loving me right now." It (the sadness) will go away like a mouse! When things occur like they have in the recent past, put your arms around you and say, "Mother is love. I am well."*

At the time I was enchanted by her reply, finding comfort in repeating her words.

As I walked along the snow-covered streets, I concluded that if Mother's response could apply to times of sadness, it could also apply to confusion or restlessness or imbalance of any kind. Thinking of my inability to concentrate and apparent writer's block, I repeated her words many times. I could readily imagine loving arms around me, and took comfort in that.

Walking along, lulled by the rhythmic motion of my footsteps crunching on the frozen snow, it suddenly dawned on me that I needed to be in a state of gratitude and wonderment on the walk, and for that matter, while writing. That's what was missing!

I began to focus on everything that met my eye, with wonderment and gratitude. My attention went from house to house, observing the twinkling lights interrupting the darkness, wisps of wood smoke drifting off into the atmosphere, towering trees shadowed under the streetlights, and occasional rushing streams merrily piercing the silence at the roadside. Each drew me in like the tender arms of a loving mother, as I opened my heart with gratitude and awe. Still as it was, I was witnessing life all around me. Soft as it was, I was warmed by my very breath. Calm as the night was, I was enlivened by the energy.

On I walked, feeling more at one with my surroundings, rejuvenated by the cold night air and mesmerized by this novel sense of connection. Previously unknown energy buoyed me and beckoned me to go further. Then I got it!

Simplicity is wonderment made manifest in an active form. It begins to have life, a heartbeat, an action... That was exactly what I was experiencing!

Footsteps falling rhythmically, I engaged with my environment in gratitude and wonderment, and became deeply immersed in the present moment. My entire focus was there. My mind was free of analysis, my heart open and accepting. Any sense of obligation vanished. Very little thinking occurred, other than maintaining a sense of wonderment and gratitude. I ceased searching for an answer, as I ceased formulating questions. I simply walked along the road. In so doing I narrowed my purview to wrap my world around me like a shawl.

Suddenly, yet very gently, and unmistakably I was bathed in the clarity I had been seeking for several days, and which had eluded me continuously. It was there in front of me, crystal clear, as if served to me on a platter. I was exuberant!

By completely disengaging from my mind and its logical process, and stepping into gratitude and awe, I had managed to plunge far deeper into the reservoir of innate wisdom. The clamp on my creativity vanished. Simplicity emerged when I was able to disentangle from analysis upon analysis, from preoccupation with what was not occurring as I thought it should and from the subsequent inner berating of which I was all too familiar. When I simply entered the present moment with wonderment and gratitude, love and excitement were evoked.

Mother's words came back to me:

When you are in this moment fully, and you are completely grateful, even in a silent unconscious way, you are the wisest of all beings. Your world is your servant. Your master is the wisdom within. And you are unified and whole.

In the days to follow I brought greater awareness to the present, realizing that gratitude belongs in the moment in which I am living my life. I asked myself, "Is this possible to maintain when so much of my day involves scheduling, planning ahead, meeting deadlines, and much more?" "Yes!" I concluded. I can practice gratitude and wonderment for whatever is occurring right now. I may be called upon to plan future events, however I can still keep my focus on what is developing around me. There may be a fine balance there, and that is the key.

The present moment is where I can be in complete sync with myself. Even though I may think that jumping into the future with thoughts, dreams, and desires is the way to go, if I disregard the sacred gift of the present moment and eliminate gratitude, I deny myself the growth and adventures that are meant for me now. While living in the present, in gratitude, calls forth trust as never before, something within draws me toward this way of jumping fully into the mystery of my life.

Living with gratitude, wonderment and simplicity has lifted a weight off my shoulders. I have begun to feel "with" my self, rather than on guard against my self. I am more aware of my life force. There has emerged a palpable knowing of my truth and beauty, as well as an emerging simplicity in life. The simplicity manifests in the form of greater flow with life around me.

This is the cleansing of the shadows. It is a reclaiming of my life, right here, right now, as is. It is drawing my energy to where it belongs. Even if the current moment is filled with tension or something I think I do not want, it is still "my moment". The shadows lessen in intensity because the shadows are grounded in the past. When I attempt to analyze or deny the past or project my fears onto the future, I only heighten the shadows in the present. The journey of gratitude, wonderment and simplicity releases the energy that is held within the shadows, so that I can enjoy my life right now!

To cleanse the shadows is . . . *to live in awe of all that is around you. To live in utter disbelief that such beauty can exist, including yourself. When another witnesses the beauty in you, they are witnessing the glory of love."*

How can this help but evoke wonderment and gratitude, and as Mother explained . . . *open the doorway to the truest, most authentic expression of one's inner wisdom, themselves?*

I got it! I finally figured out what Mother was trying to teach me. I lived it in that moment. I was gloriously grateful for me!

Chapter Four

Call Forth the Energy of the Sacred

Gratitude calls forth the energy of the sacred.
                                          -*Nathan*

As I was taught about gratitude, I was taught about the *four parts: intention, acceptance, peace and love.* Nathan explained that each of these can only exist with gratitude. He taught me how the four weave together, and reinforce the presence of one another. Over time I understood that as **gratitude calls forth the energy of the sacred,** it calls forth **the four parts,** which are aspects of love.

I ~ Intention

Include the whispers of Divine guidance in your life and always live from the intention to share love. - Nathan

Participating in the sessions with The Teachers was like opening a birthday gift. I had no idea what was to be given to me, until the gift was revealed. At times I was so excited about hearing the next lesson, that I could hardly contain myself! On other occasions I was nervous, particularly if I had been asked to do an assignment. Many a time I was filled with gratitude and even euphoria, as The Teachers led me through a teaching to liberate me from a burden long held.

The Teachers repeatedly conveyed to me that their intention in leading me through such a vast and varied time of teaching was one of pure love, so that I could know myself in my fullness, embody their teachings, and bring them forth into the world. Over time, I learned just how much intention is connected to love.

We will speak of intention, because intention underlies acceptance, which can create peace, which opens the door for love. Intention is the outward release of the most potent internal flow of love, however it was given to you to give to the world.

The intention to Love awakens the expression of love. The expression of love is your only job. Your purpose is to love. Your name is LOVE.

Intention is not only the act of prayer, meditation, mantra or prostration. Intention is the active principal of love in

action. It is a movement in the direction of truth or the unity of a peaceful co-existence, such that the only matter at hand is love.

You oft ask how to heal your world. I say that it is not love only unto itself that heals, but it is the <u>intention</u> to love that heals all suffering.

Clear intention, authentic intention with only the highest intention of oneness, a unity of spirits: this is the most sacred ground upon which to manifest true healing of your planet.

When you are able to place those who are suffering in a greater place than oneself, to cease your earthly desires and your grasping of worldly treasures, when you are willing to be completely present to embrace the wounded before you, when your entire being focuses on loving, nurturing, peacefully engaging with another, your intention for love becomes clear.

Kneel beside the suffering and ask, "Are you hungry?" He says "yes." Then find him food and break bread with him. Dine at the table of the unified whole. The suffering spirit and mine and the Omnipotent Force gather in sacred union, purely with the intention to love this being.

Go forth with the intention to show clearly that a heart cannot be bound by the limited thoughts of judgement and the suppression of creativity and love and unity. Awaken creativity and peace by your intention becoming directed and purposeful, focusing on how to live in love… peacefully, simply and authentically.

Your intention, the true intention to be love, is that which lives within you, that which is clearly defined from within; not given a name, a job, a degree, or coins, but a passion-filled focused display of interconnectedness of the world around and within you.

Live with the passion that is within your heart, and do nothing else. Assure that your work is what makes you smile, that your presence of peace on this planet is what makes you joyous.

Love and its expression through focused intention has its own unique expression in each individual who has entered your incarnation and its life path.

Some incarnations (people) have come for the purpose to shine love by kindness; others, laughter; others, animation, science, so many variations…the purpose is not of a job or task, but an embraced passion then focused through the intention of sharing that form of unique love with another, for the sole purpose of creating Love.

Be true to yourself. Beckon not the callings of the mind, but only that of your heart, because from the place of whatever you do, you will give to another true peace and love. Love can be taught and shared with many through the intention of living simply, peacefully and through the simplicity of accepting everyone.

As Nathan instructed me about the intricacies of intention, and intention to love, I could not help but think of moving forward in life. The minute I contemplated the intention to love, I saw myself taking steps where I had previously hesitated. Initially I recognized the need to be true to myself, to share my truth with others more than I was accustomed to doing, and giving myself much more positive regard. This took the form of gratitude. I then experienced greater openness to others, as I recovered energy previously dormant from holding myself back. I felt a release of sorts, as if by way of giving myself permission to do what I had long wanted to do.

I began to broaden my horizons, meet new people, and venture into arenas that I previously avoided. Even though I always prided myself on being a good connector, I moved beyond that. It was as if something that had been knotted in my soul became untangled. That brought me incredible relief and joy. It took me out of the woes of the past and brought me back to the present moment, with my eyes open to the future, in a place where my intention could be clear.

Nathan seemed to know exactly what I needed to hear when he told me:

The nation of humans spends far too much time looking at one another's follies when there is so much love and light demonstrated in all things. The human mind is trained to find fault, yet it is innate for you to know love.

You sit with the gifts of you, all the years of the glory of Spirit spent with you, giving you education to bring you to the point of realization and release to the most authentic expression of who you are.

Underneath your fear you are capable. Underneath your pain is joy. Underneath your trials is a teacher born to ask..."To where can I impart love now?" and to step forth and do so.

Embrace, learn from each other, give to one another, and with clear intention make manifest the highest calling... Love!

If the basis of who you are, of why you are here, is of the highest service of another and of all nations, this is called intention.

To create the world that your nation so desperately seeks, your foremost task is to look upon all of your nation and all the other nations, with love.

Live from the intention that your only will is Love, asking and seeing within you where it is you can manifest love in all situations, all ways.

Awakened intention manifests the clearest pathway available for Divine Light and Guidance to be present. Include the whispers of Divine guidance in your life and always live from the intention to share love.

Guidance is coming forth through many now and this guidance is directly from Spirit, because your people are awakening to a new awareness, because your people are releasing their pain, because your people are starting to understand that there is love, that is all, and that everything else crumbles like a castle that has fallen.

Your people are becoming more aware in many ways that each individual, gathered as a whole, can and will influence change. They do not wish to war anymore.

They do not wish to consume to such a magnitude. They wish to honor the other nations with which they co-exist. They are awakening to love.

By being love you will hear love, you will see love, you will live love. You may not even know to call it love, but you will feel peace, acceptance and a powerful intention to nourish all that is and all who are around you.

Upon receiving Nathan's teachings on intention, I could only marvel at the resources I was being given, and commit to applying them in my life.

With gratitude in my heart, I intend to live love!

II ~ *Acceptance*

> *Acceptance awakens a knowing that things are as they are because it is to be so.*
> –Nathan

Throughout my sessions with The Teachers the lessons were taught in the context of life circumstances, or in relation to something that was happening in society. Reference was often made to my home, family members, and natural surroundings. All of these provided a backdrop for the lessons taught. I have lived most of my life in a rural setting at the lakeside, amidst the rocks and trees of the boreal forest. The Teachers explained that nature is one of our greatest teachers, because of the simplicity and rhythms therein. Therefore many a teaching begins with a reference to nature. The initial teaching on acceptance is no different.

Nathan began:
When you stand upon your land in the gentle breeze in the morning, and you see the mist-filled lake, eagle with wings spread, calling your name, and you feel the warm sun or a cold breeze, and in that moment you stand in silence, no thought, just in awe, you are accepting what is in front of you. You are accepting a gift. You are accepting this as it is. You don't stand and say, "I wish the water was land, and the land was water, and I wish the sky was orange – you just accept. And you don't run and gather all your friends to come and join you. You are alone in your acceptance, while others may sleep, or another may grumble. You observe with no judgement, no thought. It is, what is in front of you.

Every morning this demonstration is given.

Acceptance is necessary to speak about before thought of peace, because non-acceptance is a barrier to peace.
"My child is sick, I accept. My mother is ill –I accept".
And in accepting I say, "Teach me, I want to learn. I don't want to have pity upon you. I want to learn from you."
Because in the energy of holding that one as a teacher, as a gift, as a divine incarnation, and then grasping that soul in that light, you've raised them high above the energy of the mass consciousness of suffering that they represent.
"I see you in the reflection of the light that is all one, and the light that is all one is <u>not</u> suffering, and is peace, and is love."

Does it mean that your heart does not call out? Does it mean that your heart does not ponder "Why?" No. These are the human quest for exploration to find the road back to peace and love, but to not have pity upon another from the place of exploration and learning.

As I listened to Nathan I immediately thought about my mother, who struggled with depression and anxiety all her life. None of us were very accepting of her situation, and only wished we could alleviate her pain, to make life easier for all of us.

"I cannot help but think how unfortunate it is that people suffer from mental illness," I ventured.

When we speak of acceptance, "unfortunate" is not the connection to acceptance.

When a person comes and the mind is ill, who says the mind is ill? The standards of normalcy, that which makes things normal, the standards of comparison, the standards of textbooks and teachers and pulpits and preachers? Is this not a person, and even farther, is this not a child as you and I? Are there parts of that child that are gifts? Yes, yes!

Perhaps in their mind they have what your books call "depression" or are they a gathering of the mass consciousness of confusion and sadness?

I was quite taken with that perspective, which seemed to soften the blow of a strictly calculated diagnosis.
 "I guess I have a difficult time accepting all that is," I replied.

When I walked the earth in early times, did I not get enraged? Did I not feel judged? My human self did, of course. But in that is the lesson of acceptance, so that peace can ensue; so that love can happen without judgment.

Ask a man in a chair that is wheeled: "Do you want me to have pity upon you? Do you want me to feel saddened by your burden?"

He will look to you and say "No. Don't see me through those eyes. See me as whole, unburdened, and in the arms of my Father who knows exactly my spirit's need."
So don't cry for the man in the wheel chair. Smile. Love him. Perhaps get a chair and wheel with him, if you feel pain about "his" burden of sadness.

Acceptance is a very foreign concept to a mind that is functioning from fear, judgment and critique, but acceptance can be a potent neutralizer of suffering and human frailties which invoke the passions of judgment and fears.

Know that acceptance is not condoning. It is Love. Acceptance is not the condoning of the frailties of another. It is not giving permission for the suffering, judgment and criticizing to continue. It is an observance of the moment that lies before you as simply that...a moment and nothing more.

Acceptance awakens a knowing that things are as they are because it is to be so, and to remember to not define the experience but to see it in a very neutral way.

Acceptance allows one to embrace the moment and simply see what you are experiencing in that moment as a complete and utter opportunity to love, rather than engage in a fear and the mind's interpretations of those fears.

As Nathan stated that . . . *acceptance can be a potent neutralizer of suffering and human frailties which invoke the passions of judgement and fears,* I made a mental association with what I have learned about the restorative justice movement.

According to the Canadian Resource Centre for Victims of Crime, in the paper "Restorative Justice in Canada",

> "Restorative Justice is not a program, but a way of looking at crime. It can be defined as a response to crime that focuses on restoring the losses suffered by victims, holding offenders accountable for the harm they have caused, and building peace within communities."

The literature goes on to explain that the emphasis is on assembling a community of people including the offender and the victim, who gather together in "circles" to deal with the offence, rather than isolating the offender in a strictly punitive manner, which most often leads to further harm.

The encounter provides opportunities for all to learn from what has occurred, to create and implement a plan for making amends and to restore offenders as whole, contributing members of society. The model is one of inclusion and community building.

The notion of community building brought to my mind Nathan's statement that *non-acceptance is a barrier to*

peace. I then realized that "building peace within communities" requires a certain degree of acceptance, or efforts toward peace could easily collapse. Since the restorative justice model is one of inclusion and community building, it makes sense that it could not be implemented successfully without a foundation of acceptance.
I pondered this further, and could easily see the far-reaching need for acceptance to take root in society, well beyond the justice circles. Why was it, though, that I could so easily become judgmental, prejudiced and wanting to discriminate against those I deemed "wrong", and undeserving of love?

Nathan expanded upon this to afford me further understanding:
Remember my beloveds, the teaching of acceptance is not about affirming that what has happened is right, just or condoned. Nay! It is saying that your face may face towards the Light or your face may be burdened by the tears of pain and suffering, but in your suffering ask yourself: "What is the pathway to love that I have been asked to share?" and move forth and share. And in this your thieves (fears) *shall become your catalyst for the most authentic expression of love offered to all Nations and to the self.*

As you are towards your own spirit, you will be to another. A focused awareness, an acceptance that you are love, you are beauty, you are perfection, you are the complete and utter potential for Love in all and that you are the Omnipotent's eyes here on this earth, will awaken the truth of who you are....Love!

Embrace your pain, accept, and you will see a common suffering and joy. Together, in commonality, all will free one another.

These very powerful words stuck a chord in me. Acceptance, whether of self, others, or circumstances, can be a tall order. I pondered Nathan's words, which went well beyond my typical notion of acceptance as one of tolerance of what may be displeasing to me, to one of the acknowledgement that I am *love, beauty, perfection, and the complete and utter potential for love in all*. We all are! What a huge departure from the norm. What a glorious revelation.

I wondered, though, what would help me grasp this truth of who I am in every fiber of my being, for I knew that if I did, it would be life altering. What would really bring this home to me? What would imbed this truth so deeply that it would influence my every thought, perception, and action? I had to find out.

For the next few days I allowed these words to reverberate in my consciousness, turning them around and around as if surveying an exquisite rose or a precious jewel. Then it came to me. Absorbing this truth that I am *love, beauty, perfection, and the complete and utter potential for love in all* was perhaps easier than I thought. It is about changing perspective based on awareness: *A focused awareness, an acceptance that you are love …*

It is about allowing myself to live by that knowledge, and to apply it. In my case, that means turning away from many of my outworn limiting beliefs, and embracing my worth, beauty, and potential.

The Teachers would often say to me, in truth and in jest, that I could be *as straight as an arrow*. They were referring to my tendency to take their message at face value. I reassured the teachers that even though it may take me awhile, I would learn what they were teaching me and I would apply it. I concluded that there are many levels to these teachings. They not only merit application, but a continual revisiting, as well, to mine their riches. In addition to that, I became aware that Spirit is continually at work in these teachings and that it is up to me to avail myself of what is being offered. Turning to the wisdom of the teachings is a means of turning to Spirit.

Mother invited me to make use of three questions on a daily basis, which would assist me to hear Spirit's prompting for the unfolding of my life. They are: (Directed to Spirit)

1. What is it that you are teaching me today?
2. What is it that I am to learn?
3. What is it that I am to apply?

I sensed immediately that asking these questions with utter sincerity would enable me to grasp the truth that: *a focused awareness, an acceptance that you are love, you are beauty, you are perfection, you are the complete and utter potential for Love in all and that you are the Omnipotent's eyes here on this earth, will awaken the truth of who you are....Love!*

I found the questions to be a beautiful and effective tool for learning and acquiring the understanding necessary to live lovingly, peacefully and with a lot more fun. For, I realized that any significant change in awareness, behavior, or lifestyle has to incorporate loving intention as well as room for Spirit to breathe in and through my life. Thinking that everything had to be up to me was an error in judgment. Thankfully so!

Mother explained that:
Everyone, everything, every moment is a teacher, is the Divine in action, is a call to your heart, is a call to peace, love and Light. Every moment and every being is a direct interaction with the Divine Light, a manifestation of your highest purpose on Earth. Awaken, live in awareness, be the observer of every moment and you will see your life unfold.

Once I began using the three questions in my daily life and applying the feedback, messages flew in from all directions. The funny thing was, I recognized that these messages had been there all along. I was only now opening the door to receive them. Once you begin to use them, get ready to rock your world!

Something else that Mother said echoed in my mind as I used the questions, and went about my daily life. She encouraged me (and all of us) to speak to The Teachers (and I believe any Divine Masters) in our hearts, as if speaking to a close friend. She emphasized the importance of speaking freely, speaking often, holding nothing back, and saying it like it is. That was enough for me! From then on I poured out my heart in the most emphatic and passionate way that I was capable of. It felt great.

The clincher for me though, in accepting that I am **love, beauty, and perfection,** was when Mother explained to me that everyone is affected by the love and acceptance I direct towards myself, or by the denial of that.

At first I thought she meant people on earth. However, her words were *all of us*, meaning those in Spirit as well. I was astounded to hear this. I always thought that the teaching on "the unified whole" referred to the unity of everyone on earth. Now I realized that that "whole" could be represented by a circle that spanned heaven and earth. It had never before dawned on me that how I feel about myself or treat myself would have an impact on those in Spirit, as well as those around me. What about all my ancestors? What about everyone's ancestors?

Suddenly I understood how we all affect one another and that, *As you are towards your own spirit you will be to another.* Immediately I felt a veil drop away. This veil was woven from the erroneous perception that led me to believe there was something of merit or even piety in ganging up upon myself, or hating myself. As The Teachers often said to me, *Folly!* Instead, exactly the opposite was taught, revered, and meant to be. With this new understanding I was able all the more to know that:
Acceptance awakens gratitude, and gratitude is the key pathway to Love.

III ~ Peace

If you live in peace, then you will live peacefully with another.
                                                            -Nathan

Early on in the teachings I was told about the need for humanity to embrace peaceful coexistence. I thought this meant we had to tone ourselves down so as to peaceably live side-by-side, however I was taught exactly the opposite. Nathan explained that:

Peace is not what your nation thinks it should be. Peace is not about calm; it is not about smiles or laughter. It can be a part of it, but is not it. There is a lot to know about peace. The number one place peace comes from is your most authentic expression of the Omnipotent Source, your own particular expression of the Divine Spark.

Nathan later asserted:
The clear intention to honour oneself with gratitude (that being the love within you) can be reflected to others around you. If you do no harm first to the self, then you will do no harm to another. If you live in peace, then you will live peacefully with another.

Peaceful coexistence can be conceived of as a beam of loving energy extending back and forth, horizontally, from person to person and a beam extending vertically back and forth from person to Spirit. The two beams intersect each other, and each of these directions is essential to the other, for they go together to make up the unified whole. A model for this is a crossbar. What I came to realize from Nathan's teachings, is that the connection already exists, even if I am not entirely aware of it. Honouring others and myself with gratitude opens my eyes to this connection, which ultimately brings about greater peace and joy in my life.

Nathan also teaches that *gratitude is a receptacle for peace and a receptacle for love.* They exist together. Gratitude holds the place for peace and love. It allows them to be. This reminds me of a flower, which is supported by the stem. The stem holds the flower in place. The flower would not exist without the stem, for the stem supports it and supplies nutrients. So too with love and peace: they require the receptacle of gratitude.

While *gratitude brings forth the only truth, love . . . the root of peace is love,* and *the secret of peace in love is simplicity.*

As I pondered Nathan's teachings I realized I needed to know more about simplicity.
Nathan explained:

It is difficult for humans to understand the simplicity of life. Humans make life complicated. It's not meant to be so. You feel you must travel farther, you must go faster, your castles must be grand, your clothes greater than a king's. How much more? Yet outside your castles, those that are of other areas of your planet show you, teach you, simplicity: the enjoyment of simplicity, of living in the rhythms of nature, of being one with all surroundings, of being connected in the land, the water, and with those that fly.

When all is unified, or as one, your Spirit, the Spirit, is free to embrace, engage, express, live and love in its most authentic form, without barrier, without resistance, without suffering.

Hearing this teaching I thought about a friend of mine, Dana. When she was growing up she wanted to go to art school. Dana's father told her she would never make a living as an artist, and encouraged her to enter the family business. This idea repulsed her. She wanted to get as far away from her homeland as she could, so opted for a career as an airline flight attendant. In so doing, she saw possibilities and she saw the world.

Dana's life path took her into many other interesting and creative endeavors, however she still did not embrace herself as an artist. Finally, at the stage in life when many have hung up their paintbrushes to dry, she plunged the depths of her artistic self. Not only did she paint, though. Dana's creativity burst forth in such a way as to birth tremendous works of art that evoke a palpable connection to Spirit.

Dana's **own particular expression of the Divine Spark**, in her artistry, was not to be extinguished. It remained alive within her even though her life meandered here and there in different directions, along the way. It endured over time.

When I am around Dana today, witnessing her passion, vibrancy, and creativity, I can feel her joy, but most significantly her tremendous peace. She will readily admit that when inspiration flows, her paintings have a life of their own. Most often she does not know what is next! Dana acknowledges that her life is indeed an adventure and that she is receptive to what is unfolding. She is **engaging in her most authentic expression of the Omnipotent Source.**

I thought about how I feel around people like Dana when Nathan explained that:
World peace begins when the world within you and the world around you, your family, your friends, your community, begin to find a commonality of love.
I wondered what else could contribute to finding *a commonality of love.*

Then one morning I awoke with a phrase running through my mind: *respecting sacred rhythms.* I liked the sound of it. At first I wondered if it was the title of an article I was to write, or a seminar to offer. I was familiar with the concept of personal rhythms, but questioned what was meant by sacred rhythms.

The next day when Nathan spoke to me, and as always, invited questions, I immediately asked, "What is meant by the phrase, "respecting sacred rhythms?"

Nathan answered:
These that you call sacred rhythms are the natural flow of the earth's energy that influences all nations that walk upon the earth. These rhythms are essential to the expression of Peace. When you walk in the same pathway as all that is around you, you become unified, whole. That unified whole is love, and that love is obtained through peace. When you sleep, when the rhythm of darkness appears, you will feel peace. When you awaken, when the rhythm of light begins, you will feel peace, when you walk with the changes, you will feel peace.
The rhythms of nature and the Divine always teach simple truths to awaken and to lead you to simplicity and an awakening to intend only love.

Do you see? It is essential to be with nature's rhythms. World peace and simplicity is acknowledged through nature: "the" primary teacher of all that is. True peace starts with simplicity.

Peace is gratitude for what is, and not more.

Once again clarity took hold of me, as I grasped what it meant to live according to the rhythms of nature and the Divine. Doing so could only bring me into alignment with the truth of myself, and therefore to experience peace. This shed further light on Nathan's teaching that:

The number one place peace comes from is your most authentic expression of the Omnipotent Source, your own particular expression of the Divine Spark.

I realized that I, like so many, had held myself back all my life from my unique expression of the Divine Spark, and therefore from the life that is mine. This is what caused the pain that I was willing to heal and be finished with now.

It was more than time to live in simplicity as Nathan taught – a simplicity that arose from living in gratitude for the fullness of myself, and nothing more; a simplicity that engendered only love, which bore the fruit of an unshakable peace.

IV ~ Love

Love is when my breath and your breath are just as important.
                                                    -Nathan

During one of the early teachings when I was still in my fledgling state, I disclosed to Nathan that I felt very awkward with love and in love. Those around me who appeared so adept at love often perplexed me. How was it that they seemed to glide along smoothly and effortlessly in a loving manner, when I was so often entangled in a myriad of emotions that impeded my way?

A lot of times I faked an expression of love. Then Nathan told that I was to be a teacher of love! Upon first hearing this, I said inwardly, "You've got to be kidding!" (Fortunately, nothing I ever thought, said, or did phased The Teachers.)

Early on, when Nathan asked me to do an outreach assignment, my initial response was to wonder if I would "do it right". Nathan asked me to be aware of my shadows of perfectionism, approval seeking and performing for acceptance, which I easily slipped into in my interactions with others when I felt insecure. I thought I had to please others in order to be loved.

Secondly, I was taught to "***Follow the clues of love.***" This very simple instruction rendered great rewards. It moved me from an external focus of trying to manipulate my environment to gain love, towards an internal focus of being motivated *by* love.

I learned that *Follow the clues of love* means to move in the direction of what I really love, where I readily experience love and even where I am surprised by love. I discovered that when I am drawn to someone or something that fuels my fire, or inner passion, I automatically express the most authentic love. I am delighted to be there, to contribute, to express my creativity, and share my gifts.

What a difference adhering to this teaching has made in my life. It has helped me relinquish a burdensome sense of obligation, follow my own rhythms more readily and love more freely. Over time, as my awareness of the teachings developed, I felt as if I was being asked to *broaden* the clues of love. In other words, I felt the impulse to be actively open and receptive to all opportunities to express love.

This spawned a question.
"Beloved Teacher," I asked, "do we need to consciously look for opportunities to show love to one another, or is it sufficient to flow with everyday life?"

Nathan replied:
It is a gathering of both, because the human mind is always in a place of seeking more knowledge. It is how the human is made. As humans, it is to live from the place of love, and what is that? That is the knowing that we are all one.

The spark of all is present and witnessing, an observer of the actions of that spark with non-judgment, and allowing one to seek more of those experiences each day.

Nathan and Mother constantly referred to the observer and the importance of stepping into the role of the observer for the purpose of moving aside from the ravages of self-judgment and condemnation (most often brought about identifying with untamed emotion) and returning to love.

The way I have become the observer is by first accepting what occurs within me in times of turmoil, and then merely observing without judgment what is going on, as if seeing it in another. The more I slip into the accepting role of the observer, the more I experience an inner clearing of thoughts and feelings which entangle me. This creates space in the form of emotional ease and then allows a sense of wellbeing to return, because acceptance (which cannot exist without gratitude, even if subtle) paves the way for peace. I refer to this process as "returning to myself".

Although not always easy to do, turning my attention to the observer and assuming that role is the quickest way for me to restore peace to a troubled heart, because it rescinds the fire of debilitating emotion and accompanying self-judgment.

Functioning as the observer reminds me of a loving parent, who is attentive to an upset child. The parent's supportive observance enables the child to feel their feelings, know they are OK, and then calm down. The child can then receive and absorb direction. Similar to a child in a state of unrest, I am at my best when I can lovingly attend to myself during times of trial, and allow myself to see beyond the emotion at hand.

When Mother taught me about being the observer, I learned that there is so much more to any situation and my reaction to any situation, than I am aware of. There is so much more *to me* than I am aware of! The fact that a strong emotion or intense reaction has arisen, is an indicator that something from within is at the surface, and in need of attention SO THAT I CAN FREE MYSELF! Engaging the observer with neutrality, yet with loving acceptance, invites the liberation.

Regardless of what comes up for me in day to day life, there is also an underlying order of things, or a bigger picture that I may not be privy to. It may include the call of my spirit that I have not heard fully. And it may be so much more than that.

 Moving beyond emotional upheaval by means of being the observer puts me in a place of readiness to receive a potential gift. It may come in the form of a freeing insight, knowledge of an aspect of myself previously concealed, or as additional energy to make a decision in the best interests of all. In other words, employing the observer "expands" us.
It is no surprise to me that being in the role of the observer invites gratitude, which invites love. The observer can be brought forth at any time, though, not just in times of turmoil. The advantage of seeing a situation through the eyes of the observer, is to move oneself away from intense emotion of any kind and return to a sense of equilibrium.

In the quote above, Nathan mentions *the spark of all is present and witnessing, an observer of the actions of that spark...* When we tap into that spark, we become predisposed not only to love, but to seek more of those experiences each day.

The more experiences you seek in life to bring forth the spark of love in another, in thyself, the richer life becomes.

For some that spark is music, for some it is building castles, training horses, or helping those on the street. We all have our places of witnessing light. Love is what we do with that, once we witness this love that creates love, unity, peace, a cohesiveness of oneness. You must cohabitate with all that interacts with your world. This is not a time of tolerance. Tolerance is a shadowed form of judgment. This is a time of embracing, unifying all as one.

'Tis also important to regard yourself with love. . . . .
If within yourself you are always looking forward to strive to be better, that perhaps you will be more loving, then there is within you a conflict of good and bad. It is always a thought to move forward, and to have more love, but to be better, to do better, 'tis not a concept that resonates with our teachings. Do you understand?

When a cup is very full you can only pour from it to share with another and to give. But when your cup is not the fullest, you always need for more; therefore you are always filling your own cup, not that of another.
Love for yourself is also expressed as the clear intention to honour, with gratitude, the love, the Light within you.

As Nathan spoke I was well aware that regarding myself with love and putting aside my striving to be better, was an area of challenge for me and for many I have known. Yet I could also see how regarding myself with love is absolutely critical in being able to love others.

Nathan expanded on that:

If I do no harm first to the self, then I will do no harm to another. If I live in peace, then I peacefully live with another. If I hunger, I know that this is felt in another. I acknowledge that all that I am, you can be and are. If I am sad, you are. If I am hostile, you are. If I am love, you are.

If you bid me to fight, I can choose to fight. I can choose to fight with the intention to love. This is a fight not of wars and enemies, but to go within and to see why it is that you have engaged a battle, and bear witness to that within me that reflects your anger, your persecution of another, and see within that frailty the original intention of all incarnations – love.

Reflect, re-arrange, relinquish and resolve within you the pain and shadows I see within you. Then, only then, can pure love peacefully exist.

Love with another is not sweet words. It is not to pamper, or to puff up another in such a way that they feel like a coddled kitten. Love is not a sweet tone of the voice, or to sound like an angel. It is an essential part of the self and will speak a truth with the greatest intention to love. Do you see?

There are those who will walk around with their hands gathered to one another placed in front of their heart, and bow their head, wish another a peaceful day, but in their heart is the fire of demons. And yet, there is another who will turn their eye, and say in a sharp manner that which burns in their heart to help another to step upon their path, for they are wailing amongst the weeds. And as they walk amongst their weeds they are begging for help, and mercy. And so the person of love will speak. For they are like taking the hand of a drowning man, and pulling him from the waters.

One day I said to Nathan, "I see so much pain and suffering around me that I wonder how I can love more?"

Nathan's reply was simple and to the point:
You often ask, "How can I help more, love more?" I say, help more – love more!

Empower love, and infiltrate everything with this love. Help all nations to focus on the knowing of love. Access your possibilities through love. Enter your heart, reflect the truths of the pain around you as being those within you, relinquish them to the Omnipotent and give love – love – love!

Simplicity is the key to a unified love, a love so essentially pure that all become sacred beacons of the Omnipotent's Light, revealing the inner Master of the Omnipotent's Light and love, and realizing your true oneness with all. If you wish to experience simplicity to achieve love and fulfillment, then walk amongst the people. Don't wear the clothes of a king, or the shield of a warrior, but wear the cloak of a simple sacred man. Let the wounded touch you. Hold them, for you are wounded too and need an embrace. When the drunkard falls, pick him up. When a child dies – bury him. When the blind man comes, love him back. He shows you your blindness to love, and gives you your vision.

Be those of whom you reject. Eat with them, drink with them. As you are with another, you are unto thyself. As you are unto thyself, you are unto another. This is the sacred path to Love, the unified whole, oneness.

This profound expose of our oneness in love brought back Nathan's earlier words:
. . . . it is to live from the place of love, and what is that? That is the knowing that we are all one.

Love is when my breath and your breath are just as important.

V ~ Celebration!

In the days and weeks to follow, I felt as if I was shedding an old skin and growing a new one. Applying even one teaching in my life made an extraordinary difference, let alone incorporating several. It wasn't easy to wriggle out of that old skin of self-judgment, denigration, insecurity and striving, but when I did, so much angst dropped away. As I consciously coupled gratitude with intention to love, acceptance, peace, and love, I felt more in touch with my inner resources of intuition and creativity than ever before. I became far more comfortable with spontaneity. I began to actually like myself in my new skin and love the life I am living!

In my very typical way, I wondered if The Teachers were fully aware of not only my progress, but also the growing joy I felt in being alive. Needless to say, they know me better than I know myself. It was no surprise, then, that Nathan brought forth the following teaching at this point.

There is so much love inside of you now. This is the important part to realize. When there is love, when there is intention, when there is peace, and when there is acceptance, and when gratitude is present, there is yet one more point that is so very important. That is the celebration of the awakening of the spirit within.
It is very simple in human terms to wish to pursue the shadows that exist. There is a tone in your world where everybody is asking themselves to fix, to fix, to correct, to fix, to make better, always searching for the shadows and the follies. Yet when one has experienced as you have, awakenings in many areas, a celebration is necessary, in order for you to feel more peace.

If one does not celebrate that which gives all those points (acceptance, intention, peace and love) that I have shared with you, what is the purpose then? I do not understand.

It is important to allow yourself to stand in front of the mirror and see the reflection of who you were. Look now in the eyes of the woman who stands before you, and see who she is. Look in those eyes and see who she was when she suffered, how she felt of love and many of the things we have discussed and you have experienced, and now, look to see who she is.

Who she is was always there, only now she is awakened. One celebrates the birth of a child. One celebrates that day every day of the year. One celebrates the newness of a relationship, or a job, but when an awakening happens even in the subtlest way, it is forgotten to celebrate.

If in this moment you remember to say, "I love you" when you did not wish to, one should celebrate. If in the moment you had a look of kindness upon another when normally you would not, there's celebration, acknowledgement, giving oneself gratitude for having the willingness to impart that which you have learned.

If in a moment you give kindness where you would once before have given anger, if in a moment you give gentleness where in a moment before you would have given harshness, if in a moment you are given understanding where you would have been given confusion, do you understand how much there is to celebrate?

"Yes, a lot!"

Celebration is an enhancement of gratitude. It only makes one desire gratitude even more and more and more. When I would look upon those who would come to me in suffering I would celebrate who they are. This is why I have chosen you to do this work, because it is very easy for you to look upon the suffering and celebrate who they are. To allow yourself to celebrate you - this is the greatest gift you can give to yourself.

"That's lovely!" I exclaimed with delight.

A celebration of you. Have you, my Beloved Student, ever given yourself a celebration party?

"No... I have not!" I said with a laugh.

We find that very important, to allow ourselves to be celebrated. That is why I would allow the fires at night with the dancing, and those who would come and allow themselves to kneel before me because they are celebrating all my work. It was not because I am arrogant, or because I wish to be knelt to or prostrated to. It's because I am, Me.

"How beautiful."

When one lives in a place of gratitude, there is awakening to the others (the four) *of which I have taught you. When one realizes the gratitude in their life, they begin to awaken to their own light. Upon awakening to that light 'tis important to celebrate every step that is taken, every part of love, kindness.*

When you celebrate you, you have celebrated all beings, all spirits, all nations, all life, all things, in all ways. When you deny that, you have not connected to that, and you have minimized the impact of the celebration.
When you look in your eyes and you say, " They are so beautiful", you are acknowledging all who were before you, all who are with you, all who are within you, all who are around you, all that is. When you celebrate that in the moment where you would have chosen hatred, you chose love, that becomes a presence in your nation, your world, and it becomes a truth.
Do you understand?

"Yes, it's very profound, very beautiful."

You, my Beloved Student, please know, when you allow yourself to ultimately love yourself, to celebrate you, even your follies and your shadows, when you allow yourself to be imperfect, you become perfect.

Celebration perpetuates gratitude. It only makes you want more gratitude. One will look upon their reflection and celebrate the beauty of who they are and immediately following is gratitude, is it not? And immediately following gratitude are those things that I have taught you.

"Oh! It all goes together beautifully!"

Yes, and this is why sometimes you humans fall, so that you can pick yourself up and celebrate, and experience all that is in my teachings. You must fall, or you cannot celebrate. There must be a birth to celebrate, must there not?

(Laughing!) "Yes, Yes!"

There must be a reason to celebrate, must there not?

"Yes, definitely!"

It's all together. You and your divine forces work together so that you have reasons to celebrate. And do you know, My Beloved, that the more you celebrate, the less you must seek things to celebrate?

"Yes, it all fits together."

It becomes one glorious party, of celebration and gratitude, and those that I have taught you, and it keeps perpetuating itself until you become bored, and yet find another reason to celebrate. You do have the capacity to have a continuous state of celebration. Some who have been in your nation have done so in times of war, starvation, violence, cleansing. Do you see? You are now privy to the key to your freedom.

(By *those that I have taught you* Nathan was referring to acceptance, peace, intention and love, and their existence with gratitude.)

"Beloved Teacher, Thank you!"

What I have given you is the four keys to self-realization. Do you see?

"Yes, I'm taking great delight in how it all comes together."

Now it comes together. So you will practice this celebration, my Beloved Student?

"Yes, and speaking of celebration, I love to dance!"

This I'm aware. Remember, celebration can also be a silent whisper, an acknowledgment that in the moment you have chosen love. And, many times it can be grand. This is for you to find.

In that very moment I knew there was nothing else for me to find. With tremendous joy and gratitude, I was already dancing!

Epilogue

The Miracle of this Book

When The Teachers suggested that I begin to bring forth the teachings via a series of e-books, I had already been working on two volumes for publication, for two years. The collection of teachings is vast and the amount of material on hand, formidable.
While I pretty well knew what was going into the two volumes, I initially had no idea what to put into the e-books. I was merely given the direction to begin by writing about gratitude. Simple, it sounded.

Easy, I thought. Piece of cake! After all, I have a good working knowledge of the teachings, and a recording of every session we've done. The only thing was, in the early stages of this process I had no idea of the extent of the project. There was little cataloging of the early teachings. I could not fathom how much material would come into my hands.

So there I was, ready to begin this e-book that you have before you, and I did not have a clue how it would come together. As with this entire process, I started out unsure of how I would arrive at my destination, but knew I would find my way. I knew The Teachers would show me how to proceed. They did exactly that, however not in the way you might think. By now our sessions were few, far between, and very brief due to a set of circumstances beyond my control. Consequently, we did not have time to interact at any length about this book. I had to learn to hear their promptings and their direction within myself.

It was, therefore, by means of an entire set of unforeseen circumstances that I found my way through this book. There were clues to be found, in abundance, if I allowed them to manifest. How I happened upon a specific teaching or quote of the teachers I will never know. How the outline came together, I do not know, because it does not reflect the order in which the teachings were presented. Yet, I do know that The Teachers are at work behind the scenes, because I could never have figured this out myself.

Certain days, when I pondered where to go next, a teaching that took place well over a year ago came to my mind. As I searched for the recording of that session, I stumbled upon another tape that gave me exactly what I needed. Connection upon connection was made as if putting together pieces of a puzzle, without the picture on the puzzle box!

During the few brief sessions that I met with The Teachers in this time period, they occasionally said something entirely unrelated to the topic at hand and I immediately knew it was to be included in this book. On other occasions, I had random meetings with people I barely knew, or did not ordinarily associate with, and in those interactions came an insight, a clue, or a demonstration of a teaching I needed to include. In my way of viewing things, there was neither rhyme nor reason to any of this!

That was the thing though. The book was not meant to come together according to my way of viewing things. There existed a complete underlying order for the creation of this book, which I was only to discover as I lived moment by moment by moment, in gratitude.

I share all of this with you because I think it has huge and valuable application for life. Having opened myself to Spirit, agreeing to the call of my heart and setting the intention to do this work, I set the stage for the spectacle to begin. Actually, I set the stage for the miracle.

In many ways, then, I had to get out of the way. I released my expectations of the process at hand and of my notion of the optimal timeframe. The important thing to note is that I lived in gratitude perpetually for myself, for The Teachers and their teachings, and for my role as a scribe in bringing them forth. Regardless of whether or not I knew what I was doing, I lived in gratitude.

Things did not always unfold the way I would have liked them to. There were moments of frustration when I wanted so badly to complete the next section, but was so restless I could hardly sit still. In those instances, I knew I had to listen to my body, change my environment and move around. As I did so, inspiration returned.

There were times when I wanted everything to move more quickly, and in a linear fashion. Yet I took great delight in the process, which was anything but straightforward. There were times when I couldn't see the forest for the trees, so to speak. The process was anything but conventional, yet I took great delight in it and could feel the hand of love guiding me.

All in all, I have learned just as much in virtue of the miraculous process of writing this book as I have in sharing the teachings. This process has been a lesson in trust, release, and allowing myself to be completely enfolded in the loving, guiding arms of Spirit. It has been about learning to accept the miracle of gratitude in its totality. There are many other miracles I have experienced as a result of applying these teachings, and I am very excited about sharing them with you in books to come.

The Miracle of Gratitude, then, and the Miracle of Life, is that Spirit is in loving communication with all of us, all the time. Gratitude **calls forth the energies of the sacred and brings forth love**, no matter what my life circumstances are, or what the past has been, no matter who or what I know, no matter how I love, no matter what I yearn for. Spirit - The Omnipotent - is loving me and communicating with me constantly, so that I may find the light in the shadows, know that I am love and live wholeheartedly as myself, as I am. It goes even further than that though.

The Teachers issue us this invitation:
Receive the miracles of gratitude. Of course, for the miracles, all we ask is a presence of hungry gratitude. This opens the gateway to our miracle. Ah! Indeed, it is glorious!

Daily Teachings

The following list of activities can be used to enhance your understanding and integration of the teachings. Each activity can be repeated.

1. Spend a day actively living in gratitude. For an entire day turn your attention to gratitude, regardless of what is occurring, how you feel, or where you are. At the end of the day take note of your experience.

2. List 22 accolades or qualities you like about yourself. If you cannot finish the list, begin again, repeating the process until you have a complete list. Observe the involvement of your mind in the process.

3. For one week watch for *the clues of love* in your life. When you feel the "pull" in the direction of love, observe, act, and take note of what emerges.

4. Write in descriptive terms *your miracle*. This is the miracle you yearn for, are ready for, and welcome into your life. Offer it to the Omnipotent and lovingly express gratitude for its unfolding.

"... It is with gratitude I live my life!"

About the Translator

Denise Appelmans began experiencing an intuitive connection with Spirit and Guides as a small child. Opening to the multidimensional world of Spirit, she experienced a vigorous ride on the roller coaster of life. What emerged was a growing passion to share the gracious wisdom of Spirit in the form of intuitive readings, and later as a translator of the teachings from the Spirit Guide, Nathan. Her work as an Intuitive is far reaching providing guidance for people from numerous countries all over the world.

Denise's background also includes over 28 years of combined traditional and alternative medical experience, along with numerous presentations and workshops offered throughout Canada and the US. Denise offers a unique blend of intuition and knowledge of the physical and Spiritual connection.

About the Scribe

Elaine Pace has been on a life-long quest for Spirit, only to discover recently that Spirit has been pursuing her, her entire life! After completing a career in community mental health and holistic therapies, in 2010, Elaine began to awaken at night to a stream of poetic words surging through her mind, that she had to immediately capture in writing. The expressive style, insights, and pronouncements came in the form of teachings that were all new to her. This continued month after month until she realized someone was speaking to, or through her.

In 2011, Elaine became acquainted with Nathan, a Spirit Guide, who taught her about love and authenticity, so that she could bring his teachings to the world. Elaine began a formative relationship as Nathan's student, preparing her for the role of Nathan's teacher. The scribe was born! Her life has not been the same since.

Elaine is eager to share the transformative teachings of love with you, and with the world. Elaine welcomes feedback from readers, and can be contacted at:

www.therelinquishment.com

About the Cover Artist

P. Danielle Tonossi, whose artist's name is PREM, is originally from the French speaking part of Switzerland. She immigrated to British Columbia, Canada, 15 years ago and now resides in the East Kootenays.

Danielle's journey in life has always been a colorful expression of Spirit, embodied in matter. Her Intuitive Visionary Art celebrates Mother Earth and the multiple aspects of the Divine Feminine. She sees each blank canvas as a portal to the depth of the inner sacred being.
For Danielle, painting is a spiritual tool for healing on a personal and collective level, as there is currently an awakening to the Wisdom and Presence of the Divine Mother. Danielle offers her Art to the world with intention, and the hope that it invites conscious awareness.

Most of Danielle's paintings are also available as prints and cards. Her inspirational deck "Multiple Womyn, who are you?" is soon to be released. Each card has a painting on one side, reflecting aspects of the Divine Feminine and an affirmation of wisdom on the other side.

Proud owners of Danielle's Art live in Canada and Europe.

To find out more about Danielle and her Art,
visit her website:

http://www.danielletonossi.com

Acknowledgment

I acknowledge with heartfelt gratitude Creator, my beloved Guide Nathan, and all who have taught me so many lessons by walking their own personal path of unfoldment...you are my sacred teachers. I am inspired by the bold courage of those who ask the question, "what is my purpose" and humbled by the raw vulnerability it takes to discover not only a purpose, but to unfold the very essence of their incarnation. The life path of being an interpreter for a Spirit Guide is a challenging one, always straddling the world of Spirit and form, but, it is a life I love and dedicate myself to....I would have it no other way!

With deep heartfelt gratitude I would like to acknowledge my beloved family, and friends for all of your love, encouragement and inspiration. To Elaine, thank you for making a dream come true.

I also would like to acknowledge my daughter to whom I am eternally grateful for her inspiration, a brilliant bright Light in my life.

- Denise Appelmans

Acknowledgements

I acknowledge the Omnipotent for the very precious gifts of breath, life, and all that has been given, to allow me to live fully and engage in this work. It is who I am!

I humbly bow to my sacred Teachers, Mother and Nathan, in profound gratitude for their eternal, loving, grace-filled presence. The application of their teachings has given me my life.

The connection with The Teachers, as I know it, would not have occurred without the unflinching dedication and tireless contribution of Denise Appelmans, Transmitter and dearest friend. Her loving support, wisdom and sense of humour throughout this process made it not only enjoyable, but also entirely possible to continue.

Kate Kroeker contributed invaluable feedback in the form of editing and encouragement. Our long time friendship did not deter her in keeping me on task, and maintaining integrity in the writing. For this I am truly grateful.
My dear friend, Cathy Hamilton, contributed a loving touch when I "could not see the forest for the trees". Her support and avid participation in working with the teachings brings immense joy.

Danielle Tonossi, our cover artist, fast became a close friend who generously donated the use of her art to bring the cover, and future book covers, to life. She is a true example of the creativity and benevolence of the Divine.

My daughter Heather has been a keen companion throughout my encounters with Nathan and Mother. She listened tirelessly, while unknowingly offering her life experience as a demonstration of the teachings. What a gift!

There are many friends and students who have offered encouragement, support and interest in my writing and teaching. They have spurred me on towards my goal, and I love them!

Last but not least, I am grateful for all those in Spirit who love me and support me in doing my work here on earth and in fully expressing myself.

Gratitude!

~ Elaine Pace

www.ingramcontent.com/pod-product-compliance
Lightning Source LLC
LaVergne TN
LVHW022112080426
835511LV00007B/773